Cacti And Succulent Plants To Make

Crochet Cactus Patterns You'll Want To Try

Copyright © 2023

All rights reserved.

DEDICATION

The author and publisher have provided this e-book to you for your personal use only. You may not make this e-book publicly available in any way. Copyright infringement is against the law. If you believe the copy of this e-book you are reading infringes on the author's copyright, please notify the publisher at: https://us.macmillan.com/piracy

Cacti And Succulent Plants To Make

Contents

Crochet A Cactus 1
Crochet A Cactus With Flowers 4
Crochet A Cactus With Red Bulb Flower 6
Crochet A Round Cactus 8
Crochet A Quadruple Cactus 10
Camilla Cactus Crochet Pattern...................... 13
Cactus Amigurumi 22
Succulent Amigurumi 27

Cacti And Succulent Plants To Make

Crochet A Cactus

Materials:

- 1 ball Phildar Cabotine colour 30

- 1 ball Phildar Phil coton 4 colour 44

- 1 ball Rico Creative Cotton Aran colour 41

- 2 balls Rico Creative Cotton Aran colour 58

- 1 ball Phildar Phil Coton 3 colour 84, 77, 34

- Crochet hook no. 2, 2,5, 3, 3,5

- Small jars 7 cm diameter, height 7 cm

- Stuffing

Stitches used:

Cacti And Succulent Plants To Make

ch = chains

sl st = slip stitch

sc = single crochet

hdc = half double crochet

dc = double crochet

Crochet pattern cactus:

Soil

Creative Cotton Aran colour 58, crochet hook 3.5mm.

The soil is worked in the same way for each potted cactus.

Start with a magic ring and work 6 sc into the ring.

Row 1: sc 2 in each st (= 12 sts).

Row 2: * sc 1, sc 2 in the next st*. Repeat ** to the end (= 18 sts).

Row 3: * sc 2, sc 2 in the next st*. Repeat ** to the end (= 24 sts).

Cacti And Succulent Plants To Make

Row 4: * sc 3, sc 2 in the next st*. Repeat ** to the end (= 30 sts).

Row 5: * sc 4, sc 2 in the next st*. Repeat ** to the end (= 36 sts).

Row 6: * sc 5, sc 2 in the next st*. Repeat ** to the end (= 42 sts).

Row 7: * sc 6, sc 2 in the next st*. Repeat ** to the end (= 48 sts).

Rows 8-11: sc 48.

Row 12: *sc 6, sc2tog*. Repeat ** to the end (=42 sts).

Row 13: *sc 5, sc2tog*. Repeat ** to the end (=36 sts).

Row 14: *sc 4, sc2tog*. Repeat ** to the end (=30 sts).

Row 15: *sc 3, sc2tog*. Repeat ** to the end (=24 sts).

Row 16: *sc 2, sc2tog*. Repeat ** to the end (=18 sts).

Stuff the ball.

Row 17: *sc 1, sc2tog*. Repeat ** to the end (=12 sts).

Row 18: sc2tog 3x (= 6 sts).

Cut the yarn, pull through the last sts and pull tight, weaving in the ends.

Crochet A Cactus With Flowers

Cactus with red flowers

Crochet a cactus with flowers

Phildar Cabotine colour 30 and crochet hook 2.5mm.

Ch 25.

Row 1: start in the 2nd ch from the hook and sc 24, 1 turning ch.

Rows 2-20: sc 24 worked in the back loop.

Crochet rows 1 and 20 together with a row of sl sts.

Cut the yarn, pull through the side sts of one open end and pull tight, weaving in the ends.

Cacti And Succulent Plants To Make

Stuff the cactus and attach to the soil in the pot.

Flowers

Phil Coton 3 colour 34, Phil Coton 3 colour 77, crochet hook 2mm

Start with a magic ring and sc 10 in the ring.

Row 1: ch 2, dc, hcd in the same st, sl st in next st, *[hdc, dc, hdc] in next st, sl st in next st*. Repeat ** 3x. Cut the yarn and pull through the loop.

Work the heart of the flower in colour 77 by embroidering a double cross stitch on top.

Attach the flowers on the cactus.

Crochet A Cactus With Red Bulb Flower

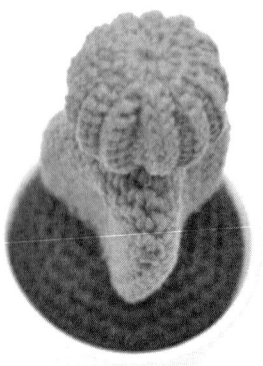

Cactus with red ball

Phildar Phil Coton 4 colour 44, crochet hook 3mm

Start with a magic ring and sc 6 in the ring.

Row 1: sc 2 in each st (= 12 sts).

Row 2: * sc 1, sc 2 in the next st*. Repeat ** to the end (= 18 sts).

Row 3: * sc 2, sc 2 in the next st*. Repeat ** to the end (= 24 sts).

Row 4: * sc 3, sc 2 in the next st*. Repeat ** to the end (= 30 sts).

Rows 5-13: sc 30. Bind off.

Cacti And Succulent Plants To Make

Shape the cactus and try to squeeze it, to give it 3 lamina. Add a little bit filling in the middle of the cactus, not too much or else it will become too round. Attach to the soil in the pot.

Red bulb flower

Phil Coton 3 colour 84, crochet hook 2.5mm.

Ch 13.

Row 1: start in the 2nd ch from the hook and sc 12, 1 turning ch

Rows 2-26: sc 12 worked in the back loop.

Crochet rows 1 and 26 together with a row of sl sts. Cut the yarn, pull through the side sts of one open end and pull tight, weaving in the ends. Stuff the ball and close up the other side as well. Attach the flower on top of the cactus.

Cacti And Succulent Plants To Make

Crochet A Round Cactus

Ball cactus

Creative Cotton Aran colour 41, crochet hook 3.5mm.

Ch 20.

Row 1: start in the 2nd ch from the hook and sc 19, 1 turning ch.

Rows 2-32: sc 19 worked in the back loop.

Crochet rows 1 and 32 together with a row of sl sts. Cut the yarn, pull through the side sts of one open end and pull tight, weaving in the ends. Stuff the ball and close up the other side as well. Attach the cactus to the soil in the pot.

Cacti And Succulent Plants To Make

Flower

Phil Coton 3 colour 77, Phil Coton 3 colour 84, crochet hook 2mm.

Start with a magic ring and sc 6 in the ring.

Rows 1-2: sc 6.

Row 3: In this row, work in the back loop only. sl st, *ch 12, sl st in the next st*, repeat ** 5x, closing the row with a sl st in the same st as where you started in row 3, but in the front loop.

Row 4: Work this row in the same sts as row 3, but in the front loops only. *ch 12, sl st in the next st*, repeat ** 5x. Cut the yarn and pull through the loop. Attach a few scraps of yarn in the heart of the flour. Attach the flower on top of the cactus.

Crochet A Quadruple Cactus

Phildar Phil Coton 4 colour 44, crochet hook 3mm.

Start with a magic ring and sc 6 in the ring.

Row 1: sc 2 in each st (= 12 sts).

Row 2: *sc 1, sc 2 in the next st*. Repeat ** to the end (= 18 sts).

Rows 3-7: sc 18 (small, cactus 1)

Rows 3-11: sc 18 (large, cactus 2)

Cacti And Succulent Plants To Make

Start with a magic ring and sc 6 in the ring.

Row 1: sc 2 in each st (= 12 sts).

Rows 2-9: sc 12 (small, cactus 3)

Rows 2-15: sc 12 (large, cactus 4)

Stuff the cacti and attach them to the soil in the pot.

Flowers

Phil Coton 3 colour 34 and 84, crochet hook 2mm.

Start with a magic ring and sc 6 in the ring with colour 34. Close the row with a sl st. Change to colour 84.

Row 1: *ch 4, start in the 2nd ch from the hook and sc 3, sl st in next st*, repeat ** 5x. Cut the yarn and pull through the loop. Attach the flowers on the cactus.

Cacti And Succulent Plants To Make

Camilla Cactus Crochet Pattern

Camilla Cactus

Here's what we used:

3.5mm hook;

Bernat handicrafter cotton (worsted weight) in Jute for the pot;

Bernat handicrafter cotton (worsted weight) in Warm Brown for the soil;

A worsted weight cotton yarn in green for the cactus;

Bernat handicrafter cotton (worsted weight) in Tangerine for the

Cacti And Succulent Plants To Make

flower petals;

Worsted weight cotton yarn in yellow for flower centre;

Safety eyes (optional);

Black yarn or embroidery/crochet thread for the mouth;

Fine or light weight pink yarn for cheeks;

A small piece of recycled plastic cut into a disc (we used a leftover strawberry container);

Stuffing;

Tapestry needle.

Terms and Special Stitches (US Terminology)

MR – Magic Ring

Slst – Slipstitch

Ch – Chain

Sc – Single Crochet

Cacti And Succulent Plants To Make

Inc – Increase. Work 2 sc into the same stitch.

Dec – Decrease. Work 2 sc together. When working in the round, I use the invisible decrease.

Hdc – Half double crochet

Dc – Double crochet

BLO – Back loops only

FLO – Front loops only

The Pot (In Jute coloured yarn):

Work in continuous rounds

Rnd 1: MR 6 sc (6 sts)

Rnd 2: Inc around (12 sts)

Rnd 3: Sc, inc. Repeat around (18 sts)

Rnd 4: Sc 2, inc. Repeat around (24 sts)

Rnd 5: Sc 3, inc. Repeat around (30 sts)

Rnd 6: Sc 4, inc. Repeat around (36 sts)

Rnd 7: In BLO, sc around (36 sts)

Rnds 8-9: Sc around (36 sts)

Rnd 10: Sc 11, inc. Repeat around (39 sts)

Rnds 11-12: Sc around (39 sts)

Rnd 13: Sc 12, inc. Repeat around (42 sts)

Rnds 14-16: Sc around (42 sts)

Rnd 17: In FLO, dc around (42 sts).

Join and tie off. Fold down the row of dc sts to act as the rim of the pot. At this point, we recommend you cut a small circular piece of plastic to insert in the bottom of the pot. This will allow the pot to sit (somewhat) evenly after stuffing.

Switch to brown yarn for the soil. Attach the yarn through the Back Loop Only of a stitch in Rnd 17. Ch 1.

Rnd 18: In BLO, sc around (42 sts)

Rnd 19: Sc 5, dec. Repeat around (36 sts)

Rnd 20: Sc 4, dec. Repeat around (30 sts)

Rnd 21: Sc 3, dec. Repeat around (24 sts)

Begin stuffing. Continue to stuff a little after each round.

Rnd 22: Sc 2, dec. Repeat around (18 sts)

Rnd 23: Sc, dec. Repeat around (12 sts)

Rnd 24: Dec around (6 sts).

Tie off leaving a tail for closing. Weave the tail in and out of the remaining 6 sts then down through the opening and out the back of the pot. Tug gently to close. Once closed, poke the tail back inside the pot using the back of your tapestry needle.

Cactus (in green yarn):

Cacti And Succulent Plants To Make

Ch 1 and turn at the end of each row

Row 1: Ch 30, sc along (29 sts)

Rows 2-21: In BLO, sc 29 (29 sts)

Join Row 1 and Row 21 together by slst together along the chains of Row 1 and the front loops of Row 21 to make a long tube. Tie off, leaving a long tail for sewing the cactus to the pot.

Cut a separate length of green yarn. With your tapestry needle, weave the yarn back and forth through the fabric around the entire circumference of the opening, a couple of cms from the top (the opposite end from the end with the yarn tail you just tied off). When you've woven the yarn all the way around, pull on the ends to close the top tightly. Tie a couple of tight knots then wrap the yarn around the opposite way and tie a couple more tight knots to secure.

And now for the trickiest part of this pattern: turn your tube inside out! Depending on how stiff your fabric is, this could be a little tricky. A good tip is to use the back of a crochet hook to help push the closed end down into the tube to turn it inside out. This is what the top should look like after turning:

Once your tube is inside out, place your safety eyes, mouth and cheeks. For the cheeks, we simply sewed some fine weight pink yarn through a stitch beneath each eye. If you prefer round cheeks: MR 5 sc, join and tie off, leaving a tail for sewing.

Stuff Camilla and then place her in the middle of the pot. Sew around the base using the green yarn tail. Continue stuffing after every few sts, if you need to.

Cactus Arm:

Row 1: Ch 15, sc along chain (14 sts)

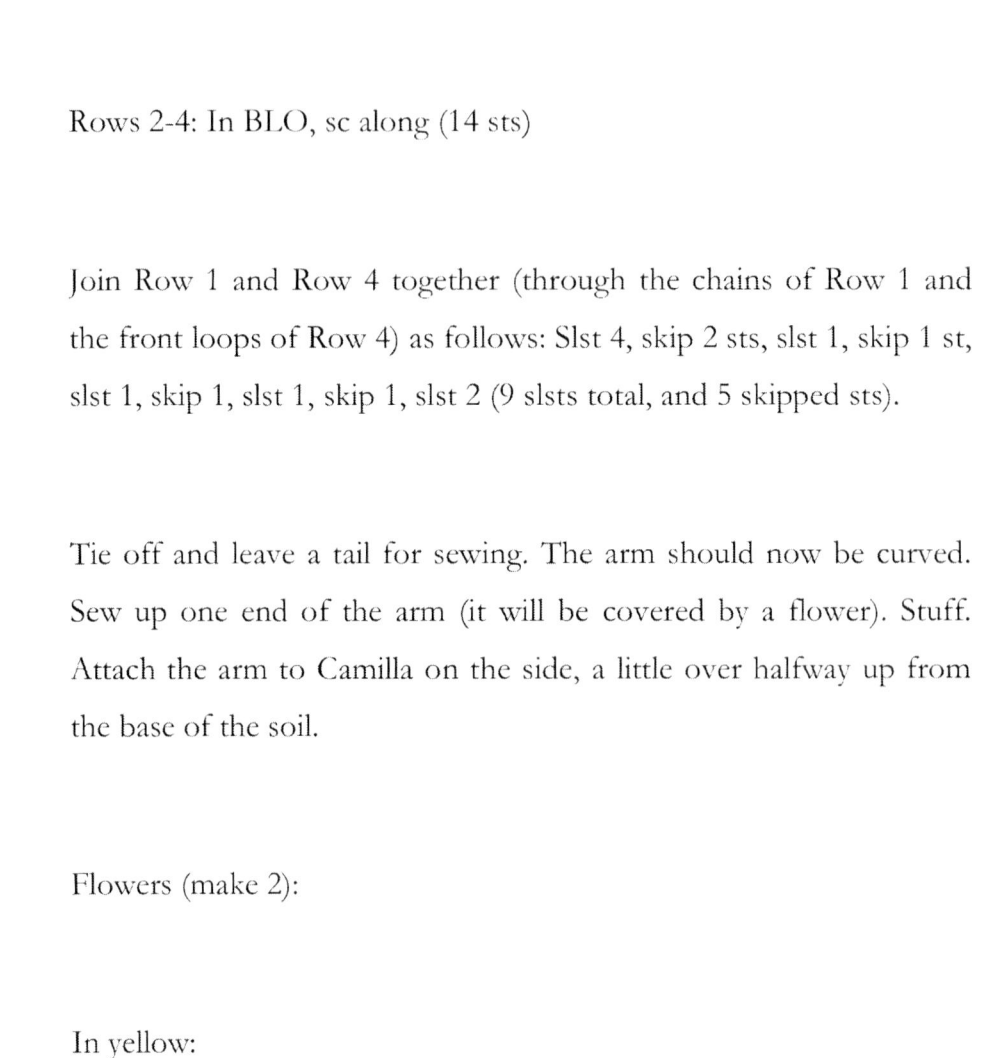

Rows 2-4: In BLO, sc along (14 sts)

Join Row 1 and Row 4 together (through the chains of Row 1 and the front loops of Row 4) as follows: Slst 4, skip 2 sts, slst 1, skip 1 st, slst 1, skip 1, slst 1, skip 1, slst 2 (9 slsts total, and 5 skipped sts).

Tie off and leave a tail for sewing. The arm should now be curved. Sew up one end of the arm (it will be covered by a flower). Stuff. Attach the arm to Camilla on the side, a little over halfway up from the base of the soil.

Flowers (make 2):

In yellow:

Cacti And Succulent Plants To Make

Rnd 1: MR 10. Join and tie off.

Switch to petal colour:

Rnd 2: [Ch 2 (counts as first hdc), dc, hdc] all in same st. Slst to next st. *[hdc, dc, hdc] all in next st, slst*. Repeat from * around for remaining 3 petals. Join and tie off, leaving a tail for sewing.

Sew one flower to the top of the arm and the other to the top of the cactus. You are done!

Enjoy!

Cacti And Succulent Plants To Make

Cactus Amigurumi

Stitches and abbreviations (US terms):

Cacti And Succulent Plants To Make

– ch: chain

– sc: single crochet

– inc: single crochet increase (sc twice into the same stitch)

– dec: single crochet decrease (work two stitches together)

Gauge and supplies:

– 3 mm (D) crochet hook

– sport weight yarn about 50 g/125 m

– brown felt

– fiberfill for stuffing

– sewing and tapestry needle

– beads, pompoms, pins…

– 4 cm (1,5 in) clay pot

It isn't necessary to use the recommended yarn and crochet hook! Using a larger crochet hook, and a suitable yarn, the amigurumi cactus will be larger preserving the same proportions.

Pattern:

rnd 1: start 6 sc in a magic ring. Work in a continuous spiral.

rnd 2: inc 6 times [12]

rnd 3: (inc, sc in next st) repeat 6 times [18]

rnd 4: (inc, sc in next 2 st) repeat 6 times [24]

rnd 5: (inc, sc in next 3 st) repeat 6 times [30]

rnd 6: (inc, sc in next 4 st) repeat 6 times [36]

rnd 7/12: sc in all 36 st

rnd 13: (dec, sc in next 4 st) repeat 6 times [30]

rnd 14: (dec, sc in next 3 st) repeat 6 times [24]

rnd 15: (dec, sc in next 2 st) repeat 6 times [18]

rnd 16: (dec, sc in next st) repeat 6 times [12]

Cacti And Succulent Plants To Make

Leave a long tail of thread, fold the work like in the pictures and lock the position with a couple of stitches for each part. Do not stuff!

Cut a circle of 10 cm (4 in) in diameter, sew a running stitch a half cm (0,4 in) from the edge, pull the thread to leave a little hole, stuffing and close.

Sew the cactus on the cloth basis and fill with beads, pompom, flowers, colored pins...

Cacti And Succulent Plants To Make

Cacti And Succulent Plants To Make

Succulent Amigurumi

Cacti And Succulent Plants To Make

Cacti And Succulent Plants To Make

Supplies:

• Yarn 4/Medium Weight in:

brown, grey, and green

Cacti And Succulent Plants To Make

- 4mm Crochet Hook
- Tapestry needle
- Scissors
- Stuffing
- 8mm safety eyes
- Black Embroidery Thread
- Cardboard

Soil:

In brown

Cacti And Succulent Plants To Make

Round 1: 6 Sc into a Magic Ring (6)

Round 2: *Inc* all around (12)

Round 3: *Inc, Sc in the next st* all around (18)

Round 4: *Inc, Sc in the next 2 st* all around (24)

Round 5: *Inc, Sc in the next 3 st* all around (30)

Round 6: *Inc, Sc in the next 4 st* all around (36)

Round 7: *Inc, Sc in the next 5 st* all around (42)

Finish off now.

Pot:

In grey or orange

Cacti And Succulent Plants To Make

Round 1: 6 Sc into a Magic Ring (6)

Round 2: *Inc* all around (12)

Round 3: *Inc, Sc in the next st* all around (18)

Round 4: *Inc, Sc in the next 2 st* all around (24)

Round 5: *Inc, Sc in the next 3 st* all around (30)

Round 6: *Inc, Sc in the next 4 st* all around (36)

Round 7: *Inc, Sc in the next 5 st* all around (42)

Round 8: In the BLO, *Sc* all around (42)

Round 9-11: In BOTH loops, *Sc* all around (42)

Now we will mark where to place the safety eyes. Add an eye stitch marker into the 15th and 19th stitch in Round 11.

Round 12-13: *Sc* all around (42)

Round 14: *Inc, Sc in the next 6 st* all around (48)

Round 15: *Sc* all around (48)

Add the eyes into the marked areas now.

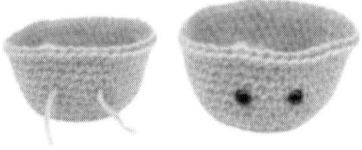

Now we will add in cardboard so the bottom and top of the pot sit flat!

Step 1. Place the pot on cardboard and trace around the entire bottom of the pot (Pic 1)

Cacti And Succulent Plants To Make

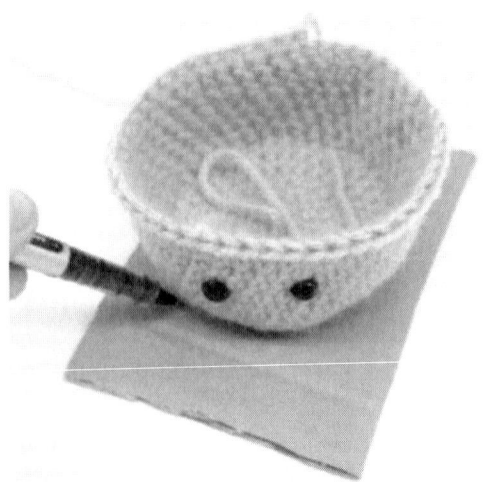

Step 2. You will have a circle (Pic 2). Cut around the circle with scissors (Pic 3-4)

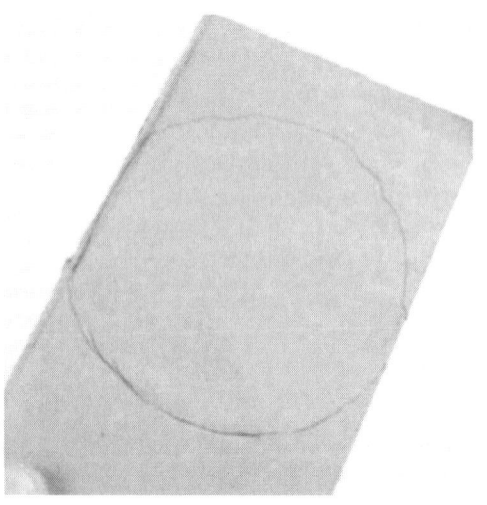

Cacti And Succulent Plants To Make

Step 3. Repeat steps 1-2 again. You will now have a total of 2 cardboard pieces. Place one piece into the bottom of the pot (Pic 5), stuff the pot firmly, then place the second piece of cardboard into the top of the pot (Pic 6).

Cacti And Succulent Plants To Make

Assembly:

Place the soil and pot together so the stitches line up as shown **(Pic**

Cacti And Succulent Plants To Make

1). Insert your hook going though both loops of the pot, and only the front loop of the soil **(Pic 2)**.

Cacti And Succulent Plants To Make

Make a single crochet (Pic 3-8). Repeat this process of going through both stitches of the pot and only the front loop of the soil. Once you have about 15 stitches left, stuff the pot (Pic 9), add in the second piece of cardboard as shown (Pic 10) and continue crocheting closed (Pic 11).

Cacti And Succulent Plants To Make

Cacti And Succulent Plants To Make

Cacti And Succulent Plants To Make

Cacti And Succulent Plants To Make

Cacti And Succulent Plants To Make

Cacti And Succulent Plants To Make

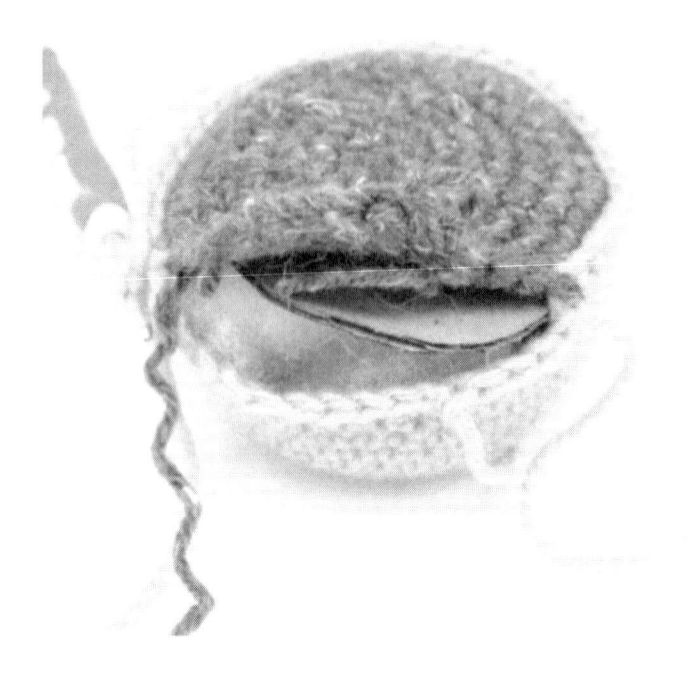

Cacti And Succulent Plants To Make

Cacti And Succulent Plants To Make

Round 16-17: *Sc* all around

Finish off, leaving a long tail for sewing. Fold the lip over and sew it down. This will create the rim of the pot. Once done, finish off and weave in ends.

Cacti And Succulent Plants To Make

Cacti And Succulent Plants To Make

Leaves:

In green

48

Cacti And Succulent Plants To Make

Row 1: Ch 56 **(Pic 1)**. Skip the 2nd ch from the hook, SlSt in the 3rd ch **(Pic 2)**. Repeat *Ch 4, SlSt in the 2nd ch from the hook, Sc in the next ch, Hdc in the next ch. Skip the next st on the Ch, SlSt in the next st on the Ch.* 5 times, **Pic 3-6**.

Cacti And Succulent Plants To Make

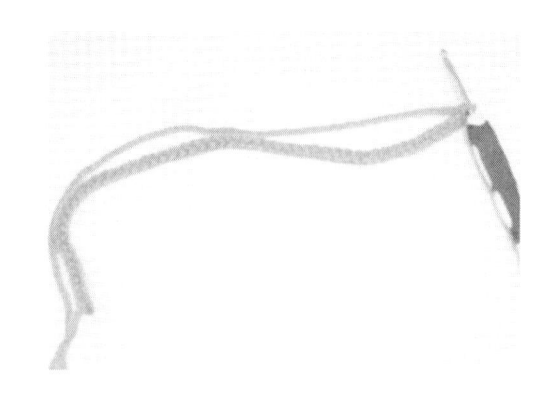

Cacti And Succulent Plants To Make

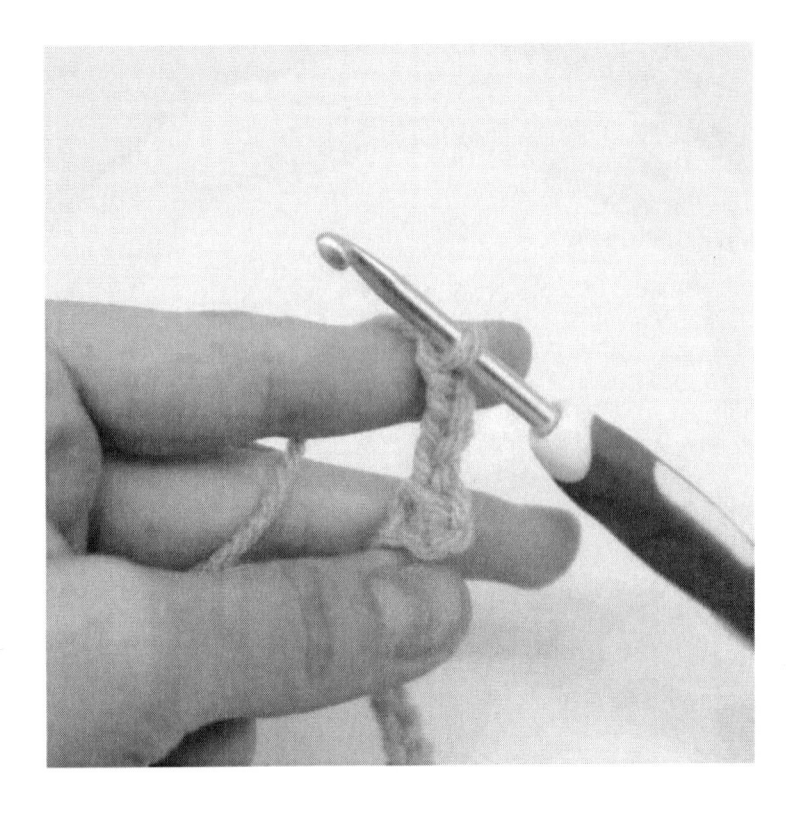

Cacti And Succulent Plants To Make

Cacti And Succulent Plants To Make

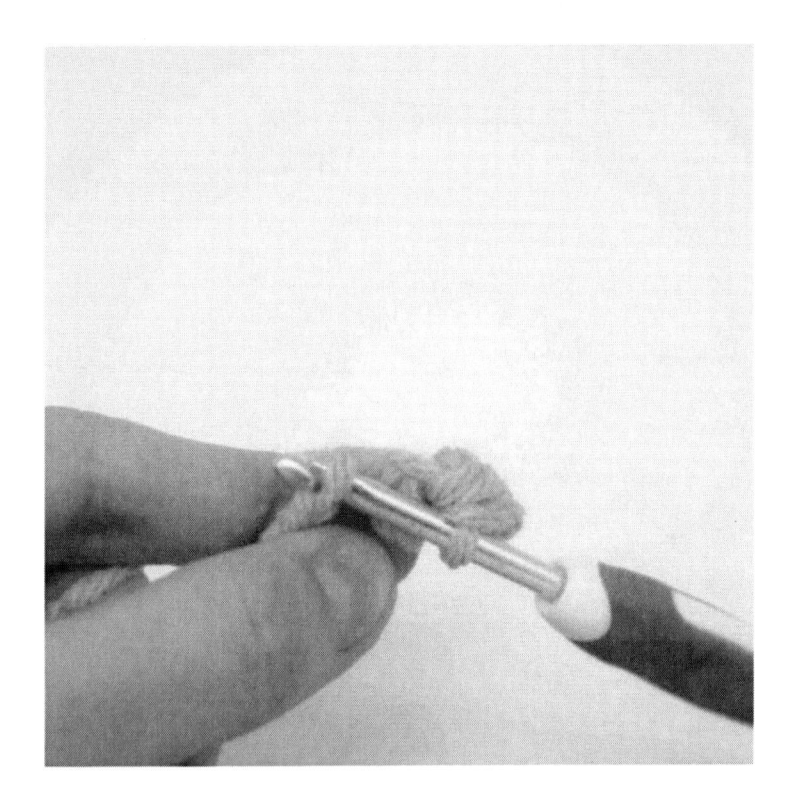

Repeat *Ch 5, SlSt in the 2nd Ch from the hook, Sc in the next ch, Hdc in the next 2 Ch. Skip the next st, SlSt in the next Ch* 2 times.

Repeat *Ch 6. SlSt in the 2nd ch. Sc next st, Hdc in the next 2 st, Dc in the next st. Skip in the next 2 st, SlSt in the next 3 st.* 13 times. Finish off, leaving a long tail for sewing. Starting with the larger side of the leaves, pin them on the outer edge in a circle. Continue

Cacti And Succulent Plants To Make

pinning the leaves down in a spiral until the smallest leaves are in the very middle (Pic 7). Once done, sew on. Weave in ends.

Smile:

In black embroidery thread

Insert needle with thread into the middle mouth area of the toy, and pull the needle out next to the toy's left eye as shown (Pic 1). Reinsert needle into the middle mouth area (Pic 2) and pull needle out next to the right eye (Pic 2). Reinsert needle into the middle mouth area and pull needle out a few stitches over. Tie the ends of thread into firm knots and bring them inside the toy to hide. This will secure the smile. Done!

Cacti And Succulent Plants To Make

Cacti And Succulent Plants To Make

Cacti And Succulent Plants To Make

Made in United States
North Haven, CT
19 April 2023